Pastor's Coach Essentials

This booklet summarizes the "essentials" or main points of the philosophy of ministry behind Pastor's Coach, and some of the resources we provide.

Pastor's Coach shaped our journey as we prepared to plant a church. Banning Liebscher, Movement Leader, Jesus Culture

Michael's Spirit-born insights make him a consummate coach to ministers. Dr. Leo Lawson President, Academic Council for Educational Accountability (ACEA)

Pastor's Coach is an incredible resource for pastors and ministry leaders. Steve Backlund, Bethel Church Global Legacy Leader, and Igniting Hope Ministries

By Dr. Michael Brodeur

Pastor's Coach
ESSENTIALS

Practical Tools for Powerful Leaders

Quintessant Media

Redding, California

Pastor's Coach Essentials

Visit our website at www.PastorsCoach.com for more information on building your church, creating culture, developing leaders and small groups, and more.

To receive a free email newsletter delivering tips, teachings and updates about Pastor's Coach and our products, register directly at www.PastorsCoach.com.

How to Use This Booklet

Welcome to the *Pastor's Coach Essentials*. This booklet contains a series of instructional essays that are part of the Pastor's Coach Church Assessment Resources.

The ten themes contained in this booklet will help pastors, leaders and church members evaluate their churches and ministries in a variety of areas, including:

- Leadership development
- Outreach
- Discipleship
- Pastoral Care
- Administration
- Supernatural ministry
- And more

This booklet will inspire internal growth within your congregation and help increase your impact in your community, city, region and nation.

Contents

INTRODUCTION

I love the Church of Jesus Christ and have spent the last forty years serving the Body of Christ in one form or another. This booklet is written as an expression of that love and my deep desire to see the Church become everything that Jesus created her to be.

Our Story

I was raised in San Francisco by counter-culture parents in the height of the hippie movement of the 60s-70s and never heard the Gospel until I started hitchhiking around the country as a teenager. After many rides with believers, I prayed to receive Christ and was discipled on the Blackfeet Indian Reservation in northern Montana. I returned to San Francisco in 1977 as part of a church planting team that provided on-the-job ministry training. After completing our training, in 1984 my wife, Diane and I started a Vineyard Church in San Francisco that soon became one of the largest churches that the city had seen in a generation. As a result, we were invited to serve as overseers in the Vineyard Movement and began coaching pastors and churches around the world.

In 2010, after twenty-five years of senior pastoral ministry and raising seven amazing children in the city, God called us into a new season of ministry - pastoring pastors and leading leaders. We turned our church over to a younger leader and moved to Redding, CA. During this reassignment time, I had the privilege of working for Jesus Culture and teaching at Bethel School of Supernatural Ministry. It was at this time that I launched Destiny Finder and began to lay the foundations for Pastor's Coach. This booklet is a small sample of the tools and resources we provide to help leaders build churches that will bring Gods' Kingdom to Earth. Thank you for joining us as we discuss what it means to be a thriving church, one that is powerfully transforming lives and impacting your region for Christ.

INTRODUCTION

The New Reformation

You and I are privileged to live in one of the most amazing seasons in human history. The Church of Jesus Christ has increased over the last 2000 years to fill the earth, and the number of unreached people groups around the world is diminishing quickly as God moves in incredible ways.

The earth's population just reached 7 billion, and many prophets and prognosticators increasingly confirm that we are on the verge of a massive great awakening. Many are prophesying a billion-soul harvest. As followers of Jesus, this could be the greatest time to be alive in all human history—and yet many churches are not ready for a great awakening of this magnitude. In order for the church to become ready, there must be a radical shift in the way we do church.

Pastor's Coach exists to prepare the Church for the coming harvest.

The key to preparing for a billion-soul harvest is the mobilization of every member for ministry. We must fulfill the outcome that Jesus envisioned "when He ascended on high, gave gifts to men, and he gave some apostles, prophets, evangelists, pastors and teachers for the equipping of the saints for the work of the ministry for the building up of the Body of Christ." (Ephesians 4:7-12) The purpose of this unique set of gifts was to equip and empower every believer to serve as a full-time minister, regardless of how an individual earns a living.

The Early Church began with an explosion of God's presence and power and multitudes were launched into Kingdom ministry. But after a few centuries, the Church became increasingly bound by religious ritual, hierarchy and tradition. After a thousand years of decline, the Protestant Reformation in the 1500s brought a measure of liberation, with the rediscovery of certain essential truths, one of which was the priesthood of every believer. Unfortunately, Martin Luther's revelation never affected the way

Church was done. The "message" changed, but the "methods of church" continued to be much the same.

To this day, most church services consist of a few leaders on a stage ministering to a congregation of mostly silent spectators. Yet God never intended for the majority of His people to live their lives as spiritual consumers, but on the contrary, God's intention is for every single member of the Church to be a world-changing child of God. We are called to be a "royal priesthood", equipped with powerful spiritual gifts and a significant calling to impact other for Christ. In order for every church to equip every member for service, we desperately need a New Reformation.

This is what we are all about. Pastor's Coach exists to help pastors build churches in which every believer will become mature in Christ and empowered to serve according to their individual gifts and callings in the Lord. We envision fully empowered people, fully equipped to be salt and light, to shine for the glory of God and bring transformation in every sphere of society. Jesus wants all believers to step into the true calling of God on their lives. This is what we call the *new reformation*, and it signals a great shift in the way we "do church."

Times Are Changing

When Jesus first used the Greek word *ecclesia*, or *church*, it was a secular word that meant "called out ones." It referred specifically to the elders who were called from the village to sit at the gates and preside on behalf of the community; they legislated righteousness and justice for the benefit of the whole village. I believe Jesus chose the word ecclesia very carefully to define our role as salt and light in a dark and flavorless world. In other words, the Church has a greater role than simply being a "feeding trough" or a "holding tank" for saved souls until they go to Heaven. Instead, it exists to be a place of training and sending, so we can go out in the name, power and wisdom of Jesus to bring transformation to the world around us, leading people into a living relationship with the living God. That is the

INTRODUCTION

apostolic model—to gather, train and send for maximum impact in the world.

This is why Jesus gave the "ascension gifts" of Ephesians 4:11, yet many leaders of the greater Body of Christ reject the existence of apostles and prophets in the Church. They mistakenly believe that these gifts passed away in the first century. As a result, these leaders only recognize the ministry of pastor, evangelist and teacher, and have neglected the other two gifts, the apostle and prophet, because they are seen as dangerous.

While it is true that these titles have sometimes been misused and misapplied, these leaders have chosen to throw the baby out with the bathwater. Yet a careful reading of the text will show us that each of these five gifts was given:
1. At the same time (the ascension of Christ),
2. For the same purpose (*the equipping of the saints*),
3. Until the same outcome is achieved (till we all come to the unity of the faith and of the knowledge of the Son of God, to a perfect man, to the measure of the stature of the fullness of Christ). Ephesians.4:13.

In fact, this passage is the ONLY time when the noun, "pastor" is used in the scripture, except when it is speaking of Jesus as the "Good Shepherd". Yet we use the word pastor all the time. On the other hand the word "apostle" is used more than one hundred times, and is used in reference to over 25 different individuals. If the role of pastor still exists, then certainly the role of apostle still exists as well.

We need to recognize and promote a healthy expression of apostolic and prophetic ministry if we ever hope to bring forth the "priesthood of every believer", and prepare the church for the coming harvest.

9

The apostle Paul goes on to say,

> "that we should no longer be children, tossed to and fro
> and carried about with every wind of doctrine, by the
> trickery of men, in the cunning craftiness of deceitful
> plotting, but Speaking the truth in love, [we are to] grow
> up in all things into Him who is the head—Christ—from
> whom the whole body, joined and knit together by what
> every joint supplies, according to the effective working
> by which every part does its share, causes growth of the
> body for the edifying of itself in love."
> — Ephesians 4:15-16

When Jesus ascended, He gave us gifts not only to equip us in
the different aspects of His ministry but also to mature us in His
nature and character. These gifts are not primarily about titles
and positions but rather about *function* and *fruit*. As these gifts
are imparted throughout the Body of Christ, every member is
matured and equipped according to the specific aspects of the
ministry of Jesus.

Quintessential Leadership: Picturing Jesus on Earth

As we recognize the importance of what some call, "the five-fold
ministry", we see that these gifts were never given to glorify
individuals but rather to create a context in which every believer
reflects an aspect of Jesus like the individual stones in a mosaic.
When they all come together they create a complete picture of
Jesus.

As Scripture says, we are one body but many members, and
each of us has a role to play in manifesting the fullness of Jesus'
ministry on earth. Why? Because God wants His "manifold
wisdom" to be "made known by the church to the principalities
and powers in the heavenly places" (Ephesians 3:10).

Ephesians 4:7-16 declares that Jesus gave gifts to equip us in all aspects of His character and ministry. A clear case can be made that this framework is the true blueprint of Heaven for the Church on earth. Many refer to this framework as the fivefold ministry, but at Pastor's Coach, we prefer to use the term *quintessential leadership.* It is one body with many members who work together to display the fullness of Jesus.

The basic concept of quintessential leadership is built on the principle of unity and diversity, which we find repeated throughout Scripture. God is one, in three persons, so the idea of unity and diversity is at the foundation of our faith. Whether we are aware of it or not, the divine concept of unity and diversity plays out in our everyday interactions and even in who we are as individuals. In particular, we see it in the ascension gifts listed in Ephesians 4:

> *He Himself gave some to be apostles, some prophets, some evangelists, and some pastors and teachers, for the equipping of the saints for the work of ministry — Ephesians 4:11*

Each of these gifts is an aspect and reflection of who Jesus is. He is the Apostle and High Priest of our faith (Hebrews 3:1). He is the Great Prophet (Deuteronomy 18:15) and the good Shepherd or pastor (John 10:11). He is the Great Teacher (Matthew 22:36) and the One sent from Heaven with good news, which also makes Him the Evangelist (Isaiah 61:1). When He gave us these five gifts, He was essentially *dividing* Himself and giving different members of His body different pieces or aspects of His own ministry.

Jesus wants to be displayed and known in the earth. However, God, in His wisdom, ordained that none of us would be able to contain or demonstrate the fullness of Jesus by ourselves. Instead, He imparted different aspects of his ministry to various members across the Body of Christ and commanded us to be in unity, like a physical body with many members. (Rom.12,

1 Cor.12)

It is as if Jesus, when He ascended on high, shown like a white light into the prism of the Church and refracted into five primary "colors" with a myriad of blended combinations.

These gifts are the essence of the very nature of Jesus, and when they work together, they create a full picture of who He is. Our value for the proper function of these five aspects of the ministry of Christ is one of the key components of Pastor's Coach. We have organized our Assessment and Training Resources to help churches grow in each of these five aspects so that Jesus would be fully manifested in our midst, so that the world would know that Jesus Christ is Lord.

With that understanding, let's take a look at the importance of leadership development as we make ourselves ready to be a part of the greatest harvest the world has ever seen.

The Importance of Leadership

Many different strategies exist for how to grow a church, but the one that stands the test of biblical scrutiny and practical results, is church growth through leadership development.

In the Gospels, Jesus had a specific strategy for changing the world and that was by building leaders.

First, He called 12 men to walk with Him and trained them to carry His ministry into the future. He did not send them to school for a couple of years, he invited them to live with Him and travel with Him as he ministered to the multitudes. His approach to training was "show and tell". He got His guys serving and ministering to others and then he would teach them during in debrief session.

As He worked with those 12, He began to focus His attention a bit more on three core leaders: Peter, James and John. In addition to the 12, He also developed a wider team of 70 others and expanded from there. Jesus developed concentric levels of leaders around Him, like the rings of a bulls-eye; He had His core team and each subsequent ring of leadership built outward from the center point.

At Pastor's Coach, we call it the principle of *concentricity*.

What does this mean for us? The average church in America has about 80-100 people. The main reason for this is that a single leader can care for only about 80 people without assistance. In order to break this barrier, the pastor needs to learn how to *lead through leaders*, a transition that is much more challenging than one might think. It requires a complete change in ministry culture and practice.

Every leader therefore has a serious choice to make: You can either *pastor people* or you can *lead leaders who will pastor others*. Jesus chose to lead leaders, and those people went out and radically changed the world.

Your Church: An Incubator for Leadership

Just before Jesus ascended into heaven, His very last words were to his friends was,

> *"Go therefore and make disciples of all the nations, baptizing them in the name of the Father and of the Son and of the Holy Spirit, teaching them to observe all things that I have commanded you; and lo, I am with you always, even to the end of the age." Matt. 28-19-20*

Jesus didn't tell us to build big buildings or to have great meetings, although there is nothing intrinsically wrong with either. The Great Commission is that we would "make disciples". The problem with this is that we have boiled disciplemaking into an 8-week class with a cookie-cutter curriculum. Yet, when

Jesus elaborates, He says, teach them to DO everything I have commanded you; this included making new disciples.

Discipleship is a massive continuum that begins the moment a person gives their life to Jesus and continues until death. We never stop growing and learning if we continue to follow the Lord. So, the Great Commission is really about raising up spiritual sons and daughters from the moment of rebirth and to equip them through all the stages of growth until they become spiritual parents in their own right. As they grow further they will eventually become spiritual grandparents overseeing younger leaders as they lead others.

In other words, the Great Commission is all about leadership development. Now some will say, "I don't feel called to be a leader." But my answer is, "the moment you said "YES" to Jesus you were automatically drafted into leadership of one kind or another. As a believer, you are the smartest person at work, you are a wise counselor to friends and family, and you most definitely are called to be a leader to your children. You may never lead hundreds, or thousands. You may only lead one-on-one or in smaller settings but don't assume therefore that you are not called to lead."

Every member of your church was designed and gifted by God to lead and serve others, and fulfill a specific destiny. *For we are His workmanship, created in Christ Jesus for good works, which God prepared beforehand that we should walk in them (Ephesians 2:10).* Therefore, one of the primary purposes of any church is to be an "Incubator" and help your members grow into the ministers that God designed them to be. We offer a set of tools and resources that will help you turn your church into a true "Destiny Incubator".

In preparation for the next Great Awakening, we need a New Reformation, in which we not only reaffirm the concept of "The priesthood of every believer," but we actually build churches that produce this outcome. In order to accomplish this, we must help every church grow in each of the five aspects of the ministry of Jesus so we can demonstrate the fullness of Him who fills all in all.

APOSTOLIC PURPOSE

We value God's blueprint for building the Church and transforming the world.

> *Now, therefore, you are no longer strangers and foreigners, but fellow citizens with the saints and members of the household of God, having been built on the foundation of the apostles and prophets, Jesus Christ Himself being the chief cornerstone.*
> *— Ephesians 2:19-20*

God's plan to change the world began the same way He created the world. Adam and Eve were given a mandate to "be fruitful and multiply. Fill the earth and subdue it," and in response, they gave birth to children, who gave birth to children ultimately to fill the earth and steward the planet on God's behalf.

In the New Covenant, we have a mandate to make disciples, which is similar to the mandate found in Genesis 1. However, instead of filling and subduing the earth through biological family, we are called to extend God's kingdom through spiritual family and sons and daughters who are born again by the Spirit of God. These people are then raised and trained up in "households" of local church expression, and empowered to bear fruit. They are sent out to have sons and daughters of their own in the various spheres of society to which God has called them. That is the essence of the apostolic calling. In its purest definition, the definition of the apostolic gifting is "a sent one who sends"—a spiritual parent who raises up sons and daughters according to God's design and sends them out to fulfill their destinies.

What Is an Apostle?

Most of us think of apostles as people who plant churches, heal the sick and so forth, and yes, apostles are called to function in the full authority of Jesus. However, the emphasis in Ephesians 4 is not so much on the *function* of an apostle but on the apostle's role as an *equipper*. In other words, the apostle is meant to impart his gift to the larger group.

As Paul describes in 1 Corinthians 3:10, apostles are master builders who release other people to contribute to the building according to their unique gifts and callings in Christ. Apostles lay foundations and establish the "footprint" of what the Body of Christ is supposed to look like.

As we look at the apostolic gift, we need to remember that it expresses itself in different models in different people. We could think of them as different apostolic "flavors." Peter was different than Paul. Paul was different than Barnabas. The apostolic calling is not a one-size-fits-all calling. Instead, there are *prophetic* apostles, *pastoral* apostles, *teaching* apostles and so forth—these are people who have true apostolic callings but express them with a different style and flavor than an apostolic leader in a different movement.

What If You're Not Apostolic?

Not every senior leader is called to be an apostle or will function with apostolic leadership as his or her primary gift. But that doesn't need to hinder this leader from being apostolic. The five aspects of Christ (the fivefold or quintessential leadership gifts) were given to equip the Church for the work of the ministry. Sometimes we make the mistake of glorifying the individuals who function in the fivefold gifts so much, that we forget Ephesians 4 is all about empowering *others* into fruitful ministry. Because these ministry gifts are about equipping the body, all of us are able to draw from these leaders the resources we need to fulfill our roles more effectively. In other words, even if we aren't called to be apostles, we can still draw from apostolic leaders a measure of "apostolic grace" that empowers us to be more apostolic than we would be otherwise.

Let's say Steve is a pastor with a pastor's wiring. He is a connector and a shepherd who isn't heavily gifted in the apostolic. However, he wants to grow in this area, so he spends a lot of time reading apostolic biographies, meeting with apostolic leaders and attending conferences where apostolic leaders are speaking. Every time he is around someone who is thinking and acting in an apostolic fashion, it impacts him and enhances his ability to function more apostolically. Steve doesn't have to be called as an apostle to be apostolic. He merely has to receive impartation and equipping from true apostolic leaders. We need to be exposed to every aspect of Christ so we can be enhanced in all aspects His life and ministry.

As another example, you have the ability to appropriate and apply what you are reading right now. A lot of what we are teaching you through Pastor's Coach is apostolic in nature. You may not be naturally wired to think or act in an apostolic way, but your exposure to this material and your willingness to learn can help you be more apostolic than you would be naturally.

What About Now?

There is nothing new about the apostolic gift. It has functioned in every generation since the time of Jesus. Most apostles throughout history functioned under the title of Pastor, but demonstrated their apostolic gifting by building strong, reproducing churches and ministries. Some were missionaries who went out and laid a foundation where no other foundation had ever been laid, and some expressed themselves in other unique ways. The gift has always existed. If apostles and prophets have "passed away," as some believe, it must be that teachers and pastors have passed away as well.

One final note here before we move on: Even though we are in a massive transition from pastoral to apostolic, we cannot minimize the importance of the pastoral role. It is absolutely essential for every healthy church to have thriving community and relationship between its members. We need both gifts—the apostle and the pastor—to build a thriving church; however, according to

APOSTOLIC PURPOSE

1 Corinthians 12:28, primary leadership should always be apostolic.

How to Build Apostolic Vision

Our vision is clearly stated and is understood by all our members.

> *Where there is no revelation [vision], the people cast off restraint.*
> — *Proverbs 29:18*

Apostolic vision comes from fasting and prayer; seeking the Lord; listening to His voice; and paying attention to prophetic dreams, visions and other encounters. Paul said he wasn't disobedient to "the heavenly vision" he received at the moment of his salvation (Acts 26:19). Much of his ministry over the next few decades was inaugurated the moment Jesus encountered him on the road to Damascus. One encounter with God, and everything changed in Paul's life. How do we promote an apostolic vision in our churches?

1. Communicate the vision.
Paul described himself as a *master builder* (1 Corinthians 3:10). In essence, this is a general contractor who has primary responsibility for the "blueprint" of Heaven (that is, the God-given vision). The primary responsibility of a leader is to communicate that vision. It is also the master builder's responsibility to enlist and train gifted sub-contractors. The general contractor does not need to be the best framer, plumber or electrician, but he needs to know enough about all dimensions of building to lead other specialists as they follow the blueprint and fulfill each of their roles.

2. Break it down.
As the master builder, the apostolic leader is the custodian of the blueprint. He needs to know how to procure all the needed resources to build the house. He also needs to know how to

assign specific responsibilities to his subs and workers. An apostolic leader needs to know how to set goals, determine priorities and objectives and then mobilize the team to fulfill these things.

3. Celebrate people who are doing apostolic things.
As leaders, we have an amazing opportunity to mirror the heart of Jesus as we encourage those around us to go forth and build. An apostolic leader is the source of vision, momentum and quality control. He is also responsible to be a source of hope and encouragement to every team member. This is even more true in the midst of inevitable challenges and disappointments.

How to Build Apostolic Culture

We have clarified our values and cultivated a strong Kingdom culture.

> *"Heaven is My throne,*
> *And earth is My footstool.*
> *Where is the house that you will build Me?*
> *And where is the place of My rest?"*
> *— Isaiah 66:1*

Culture is the shared values, priorities and practices, along with the traditions, symbols and expressions that unite a community and connect that community to its past, present and future. Culture is to community what habit is to an individual. Culture is like the banks of a river. Where the banks are strong and stable, they *channel* the river's flow, taking it where it needs to go. Once it is built, culture has an amazing power to steer large groups in the direction you desire to go. Apostolic Culture develops spiritual children into fully functioning Kingdom Adults who know their identity, practice community, embrace maturity, grow in responsibility and fulfill their destinies.

APOSTOLIC PURPOSE

If you want to build an apostolic culture in your church, consider the following steps:

1. Personify the culture you are building.
Living things grow from the inside out. This is why it's important for every change of a leader's church culture to begin in the life of the leader first. The desire to develop people into the fullness of Christ needs to be a central point in your values, priorities and practices as a leader.

2. Infuse that culture into your primary team.
Once culture has been embraced by the primary leader, it is time to introduce the new vision to your team. Infuse your core team with the values and priorities that will help them carry the apostolic culture into the congregation. Model this new culture to the team by serving them in the exact way that you want them to minister to the church.

3. Bring the culture to your congregation.
An apostolic culture thrives when its individual members discover who they are in Christ and are empowered and equipped to impact the world around them. This is accomplished through teaching and testimony. Make sure you celebrate those who are walking in the culture you are trying to build. Celebrate in public and correct in private.

How to Build Apostolic Lifestyle

Our members embrace their responsibility to serve God and others.

> *"I will put My law in their minds, and write it on their hearts; and I will be their God, and they shall be My people."*
> — *Jeremiah 31:33*

As your church adopts an apostolic lifestyle, a set of practices begins to emerge that reflects the things your church does naturally. You don't do them because you are *told* to do them or because you have a program set up that helps you do them. Instead, you do them naturally because you love Jesus, His Word and His purposes, and these things are deeply entrenched in your heart as a community. The values you embraced have become a way of life for you. The following steps will help you build an apostolic lifestyle in your church.

1. Declare the vision of an apostolic lifestyle.
An apostolic lifestyle is all about the individuals and community organizing their lives to foster personal growth, ministry development and going out into the world to bring Heaven to earth.

2. Identify and remove challenges.
What do you value? How do you prioritize those values? Look at how you manage your money, spend your time and allocate your talents. Are you giving your best for the purposes God created?

3. Celebrate the personal and organizational victories.
Encourage your church to build an apostolic lifestyle, and celebrate those who are organizing their lives in the right direction. Recognize the efforts that different groups and ministries are making to create an apostolic church.

How to Build Apostolic Structure

Multiplication of new ministry is built into all we do.

> Therefore, holy brethren, partakers of the heavenly calling, consider the Apostle and High Priest of our confession, Christ Jesus.
> — Hebrews 3:1

Ministries are like vehicles. They work well for a time and then you trade them in for a newer model—you don't expect a car to last forever. The same thing is true with ministries. We can't be afraid to let a ministry die. "Supernatural selection" is the survival of the favored things. God will innovate certain things at certain stages of time; He will let that dynamic run its course and then move on to something new. Therefore, we always want to be sure new "babies" are being born—that new ministries are being developed. The apostolic impulse is to help people discover and function in who they are. Out of necessity, those people will then join existing ministries where they can be fruitful.

1. Articulate your vision and submit it for counsel.
Begin with the end in mind. What is your goal?

2. Share the vision and build a team.
A healthy team is absolutely essential for a successful ministry. Share your vision with those you believe God has called to walk with you and invite them into the building process.

3. Launch the ministry and make adjustments as you go.
After each event, evaluate with your team.

How to Build Apostolic Leadership

We effectively train and release emerging apostolic leaders.

> "Therefore whoever hears these sayings of Mine, and does them, I will liken him to a wise man who built his house on the rock: and the rain descended, the floods came, and the winds blew and beat on that house; and it did not fall, for it was founded on the rock."
> — Matthew 7:24-25

The power of apostolic ministry in your church depends on your ability, as a primary leader, to identify emerging apostolic leaders and mentor them into their roles. As they pioneer new ministries, they raise up the next generation of apostolic leaders and complete the cycle—spiritual children mature into spiritual adults, who produce more spiritual children.

As a leader, look at your congregation and identify which individuals have an apostolic calling. You could use a gift assessment tool like the one we offer at **www.DestinyFinder.com** to help narrow down and identify the gifts and callings of individuals in your church.

Raising Up Leaders

At Pastor's Coach, we have five steps to leading leaders. We adapted this list from John Wimber's teaching on development.

1. Identify
Begin by thinking about what your team needs.

2. Recruit
Spend time with the people God highlights to you. Feel them out to see if they share your vision and values and start inviting them to do things with you.

3. Train
Spend time with your people; share your vision, values and goals with them; and train them in the specific functions you are asking them to carry out.

4. Deploy
Don't give them meaningless tasks that don't allow them to be leaders; instead, trust them to lead in your absence and do what you would do in that situation.

5. Support: Monitor and Nurture
Monitor your deployed leaders' activity in a way that builds them up and helps them go even further. *Nurturing* is essentially pastoral care. Most burnout occurs when monitoring and nurturing are lacking.

If you walk out these five steps with your leaders, you will have an ever-multiplying leadership team that will carry your pastoral care to a growing congregation.

PROPHETIC POWER

Every Church is called by God to express the Prophetic Purpose of Jesus. Therefore, we value God's presence and power and welcome God to move in our midst.

Whom have I in heaven but You?
And there is none upon earth that I desire besides You.
— Psalm 73:25

Then he said to Him, "If Your Presence does not go with us, do not bring us up from here."
— Exodus 33:15

You shall receive Power after the Holy Spirit has come upon you and you shall be witnesses unto me in Jerusalem, Judea, Samaria, and into the uttermost parts of the earth.
— Acts. 1

Without the presence and power of God, Christianity is just another religion. As followers of Jesus, we are born again and indwelt by the Spirit of the Living God, and therefore we are a prophetic people. In the last 2000 years, not a single season passed in which the earth failed to experience some move of God's Spirit.

Moses wished that all God's people were prophets (Numbers 11:29). As we fast forward to the coming of Christ and the New Covenant, that prayer is fulfilled:

"I will pour out of My Spirit on all flesh;
Your sons and your daughters shall prophesy,
Your young men shall see visions,
Your old men shall dream dreams."
— Acts 2:17

Every single person who is filled with the Spirit is prophetic by nature. Traditionally, there are three "levels" of prophetic gifting commonly identified as 1) the gift of prophecy, 2) the ministry of prophecy and 3) the office of a prophet.

First is the basic ability to prophesy, which we all have. All of us can hear God's voice and be led by His Spirit. Even if we don't consider ourselves "prophetic," we can expand our ability to hear His voice by studying the prophetic, learning *how* to hear Him and being around prophetic people. We need to be exposed to every aspect of Christ so we can be enhanced in all His aspects.

The second level of prophetic gifting is the ministry of prophecy, which is the consistent gift of prophecy functioning in an individual. The people around that person and the church he attends recognize he has a prophetic gift that is more visible than most.

The third level of prophetic gifting is the *office* of prophet. These are the people whose prophetic abilities have been refined, proven and confirmed over a period of years. They are known as prophets, and their gift is recognizable, and endorsable, by the greater Body of Christ. The office of the prophet is reserved for those God has called to function in prophecy at a high level of influence and accuracy.

Those are the three levels of the prophetic gift working in the local Body of Christ. No matter where you fall within these three levels, you can expand your gift and learn to hear God's voice more clearly and frequently.

The Key to the Prophetic Gift

As Christians who want to hear God's voice, we value the prophetic and desire to foster a prophetic reality in our midst— but how? Many of us have experienced how overemphasizing the prophetic can be harmful to God's greater purposes. We've all heard of people who were so "heavenly minded" that they were no earthly good. We've seen prophetic gifts used inappropriately in one way or another. Yet this gift is indispensible for the full measure of Christ to be manifested in the Church.

Scripture identifies a dynamic partnership between the prophetic and apostolic gifts and is foundational to a healthy expression of Christ (Ephesians 2:20). The prophet needs the apostle and the apostle needs the prophet in order for both to operate at their best. The prophetic gift is brought into right relationship with the body when it is paired with the apostolic gift. Prophets are strong in revelation, while apostles are generally stronger in wisdom and application. This doesn't mean that prophets don't have wisdom or that apostles don't have revelation, but all of us have strengths God gave us to steward.

The prophet without an apostle will tend to produce a realm of *fantasy* (subjective impressions without structure), while the apostle without the prophet will tend to produce a realm of *factory* (structures without the Spirit). We need both gifts operating together to produce true spiritual family. The relationship between the prophet and apostle is a tangible manifestation of the spirit of wisdom and revelation (Ephesians1:15).

How to Build Prophetic Vision

Intercession, prayer and hearing from God are priorities in all we do.

> *You are my portion, O Lord;*
> *I have said that I would keep Your words.*
> *— Psalm 119:57*

Prophetic vision is first of all about God's presence. We are called to be people who foster the very presence of God in our congregations, learning how to favor and interact with His presence through worship, prayer, waiting on Him, soaking and biblical meditation. In the Old Testament, the Holy Spirit came upon certain individuals only, but under the New Covenant, if you are born again and have the Spirit of God dwelling in you, you have entered a new prophetic dimension.

1. Make the vision practical.
Practical simply means that you teach on it regularly and reinforce its different aspects within your church. Try to give your congregation a picture of what a church filled with the Spirit looks like.

2. Model the vision.
As a leader in your church, are you walking in the prophetic? Are you cultivating and nurturing it?

3. Make the prophetic vision a priority for your staff and church.
If you give honor to God's presence, it will gradually increase in your midst, and the people you're leading will find a greater and greater experience of the presence and power of God.

How to Build Prophetic Culture

We commit time, energy and resource to pursuing God's presence.

> *Surely the Lord God does nothing,*
> *Unless He reveals His secret to His servants the*
> *prophets.*
> *— Amos 3:7*

The best way to increase your church's experience of God's presence and power is by building a prophetic culture. John Wimber was convinced that the healthiest churches were grown from the inside out. What are your values—the things you really care about? All culture emerges out of values, but there is a difference between *aspired* values and *actual* values. When values are combined with priorities (how you allocate your time, energy and money) and practices (what you do in your daily life), they become a cultural component.

PROPHETIC POWER

1. Personify your value for the presence and power of God.
How much time do you devote to worship, ministry and people
who are being trained to minister to one another? Where is most
of your energy going?

2. Incorporate the prophetic deeply into your team.
Everything you want to bring to your church has to be real inside
of you and your team before you can bring it out.

3. Make the prophetic a natural part of your church body.
Keep your vision in front of the people and constantly refocus
them on the church's values, priorities and practices.

How to Build Prophetic Lifestyle

We cultivate an environment where people encounter God.

> *Prophecy never came by the will of man, but holy men of
> God spoke as they were moved by the Holy Spirit.*
> — 2 Peter 1:21

The true test of your effectiveness in building a prophetic culture
is that your members become more "naturally supernatural." As
your church adopts a prophetic lifestyle, a set of practices begins
to emerge that reflects the things your church does naturally.
You don't do them because you are *told* to do them or because
you have a program set up that helps you do them. Instead, you
do them because you love Jesus, His Word and His purposes,
and these things are deeply entrenched in your heart as a
community. The values you embraced have become a way of life
for you.

1. Promote your vision.
The first step in building a prophetic lifestyle is knowing your
vision for the prophetic and running with it. What do you want to
see happen in your church?

2. Identify and remove challenges.
Begin to identify challenges that hinder you and your church from living a prophetic lifestyle.

3. Celebrate church on a consistent basis.
Preach on the prophetic, and encourage a prophetic reality in every context.

How to Build Prophetic Structure

We build ministries that facilitate the work of the Holy Spirit.

> *And so we have the prophetic word confirmed, which you do well to heed as a light that shines in a dark place, until the day dawns and the morning star rises in your hearts.*
> — *2 Peter 1:19*

Structure sounds like a swear word to many people, especially those who love the presence and power of God. We tend to pit the idea of *structure* against the idea of *spontaneity* when, in actuality, there is no battle between the two. It's like drinking a cup of coffee—we have to have a structure (the cup) in which to hold the coffee and convey it to our mouths. Without that structure, we wouldn't be able to enjoy the coffee. Jesus used the term *wineskin* to describe such a structure and said we needed new wineskins for new wine. As a pastor, if you are trying to bring a greater expression of God's presence and power to your church, you need to build "wineskins" that will support it.

Suggested Prophetic Ministries:
    1. Worship
    2. Intercession
    3. Prophetic teams and community

The key to maintaining prophetic growth is reinforcing your vision for it again and again. Tell your church, "These are our values. We're making prophetic growth a primary purpose of our gatherings, so we can experience more of God's presence and power."

How to Build Prophetic Leadership

We effectively train, release and mentor new prophetic leaders.

> *Blessed is he who reads and those who hear the words of this prophecy, and keep those things which are written in it; for the time is near.*
> *— Revelation 1:3*

New prophetic leaders come out of incubators such as small groups, worship teams, prophetic communities and intercessory teams. It is important to raise them up and work with them to release new expressions of prophetic ministry in your world. Once a quarter or even bimonthly, have an "altar call" for those you would consider to be prophetic: people who are hearing God's voice, receiving words of knowledge and wisdom, having dreams and visions and so forth. Begin to take note of those individuals, and gather them together from time to time and pour into them. Make sure they are part of your overall leadership structure, that they value the whole Body of Christ and that they are part of small groups. They need to be given permission to function prophetically in their small groups and ministry teams in addition to anything else they may be doing. Request and try to maintain permission to speak into their lives, providing guidance and correction when needed.

As you do these things, you will harvest a "crop" of new prophetic gifting that will further prophetic growth in your church.

EVANGELISTIC PASSION

We value the gospel of the Kingdom revealed in the words and works of Jesus.

> *"For the Son of Man has come to seek and to save that which was lost."*
> — *Luke 19:10*

A few years ago, we came across a shocking statistic. A study reported that not a single U.S. county was experiencing conversion-based church growth that exceeded the region's population growth. In other words, we may be gaining new members as people move into our region or transfer directly from other churches—but generally speaking, we are not doing a good job of winning the lost.

Why is that? As leaders, how can we make evangelism a more prominent expression in our congregations?

True Revival and People's Souls

People have different thoughts on the topic of evangelism. One teaching says that we don't want unbelievers to be reduced to "marks" or conquests; however, the bottom line is that they *are* our targets. We genuinely care about souls because their eternal destiny hangs in the balance. When Jesus looked upon the multitude, He was moved with compassion, seeing them weary and scattered like sheep without a shepherd (Matthew 9:36). Most of us don't see souls the way Jesus sees souls. We need to allow our hearts to feel what Jesus feels and be moved with compassion.

Another teaching incorporates the seven "mountains" of society and *Victorious Eschatology* (2007). We are called to occupy until Jesus comes and impact every sphere of society; it is true that as the reign and peace of Jesus continually increase (Isaiah 9:7), we can expect His Church to grow and become brighter, even if the world gets darker. However, the power of Jesus to change the world does not relieve us from the urgency of the times. A revival without souls is merely a renewal; we cannot have true revival without souls. Ultimately, the mandate to be fruitful, multiply, fill the earth and subdue it is still on the table. We are no longer dealing with *physical* regeneration but *spiritual* regeneration as God works through the Church.

How Do We Reach People for Jesus?

Not every leader in a church is called to be an evangelist or will function with evangelism as her primary gift, but that doesn't need to hinder the leader from being evangelistic. Even if we don't consider ourselves to be evangelists, we can expand our ability in this area by studying evangelism, learning *how* to evangelize and being around evangelistic people.

Here are a few thoughts on how to reach the unreached:
1. Help outsiders understand your world (see 1 Corinthians 12-14). Every church needs to help visitors and new members take incremental steps to greater experience and encounter with God's presence. Train your people how to invite their unsaved friends and prepare them for a supernatural environment.

2. Avoid "hype" and the appearance of hype as much as possible. Make a point of incarnating Jesus in a manner consistent with the people of your city or region, which will bring them to Christ with the fewest obstacles possible.

3. Train your people to lead others to Jesus. This can be modeled publicly in altar calls; taught in classes; and even learned in basic role-playing opportunities, where one person pretends to be the minister and the other the seeker. Consider using a simple tool like the Four Spiritual Laws as a template for personal evangelism.

4. Identify and raise up new evangelists to lead the way in reaching the unreached and to equip the saints for the work of

ministry. You can identify them by preaching on the subject and calling forward those whose hearts are burning to respond. You could also use a gift discovery tool such as www.DestinyFinder.com to help in the identification process. Once these individuals are identified, pull them aside to form an evangelistic leadership core team, who will help you write training materials for the whole church and impart their gifts to others.

How to Build Evangelistic Vision

Our members are motivated to share their faith with the lost.

> Then Jesus went about all the cities and villages, teaching in their synagogues, preaching the gospel of the kingdom, and healing every sickness and every disease among the people. But when He saw the multitudes, He was moved with compassion for them...
> — Matthew 9:35-36

Many churches we coach are concerned because they see *transfer* growth but not *conversion* growth. Ultimately, this comes down to a matter of vision. We need to have a vision for souls if we are going to reach the people around us. The desire to reach the lost begins in the heart; our hearts need to break over those who don't know Jesus. A soul that dies without God's salvation is a soul that is eternally separated from Him—this should grip us at an intense level and compel us to go out into the world to reveal His love.

1. Make the vision practical.
The vision for souls is birthed in the heart of the lead pastor or couple. Even if you aren't called as an evangelist, the burden for souls starts in you and then spreads to the leadership team. Give people simple ways to talk about their faith.

2. Show people what the vision looks like.

EVANGELISTIC PASSION

Incorporate evangelism deeply into your own life. Do you as a leader actively share your faith? Do you spend any quality time with unbelievers?

3. Make evangelism a priority for your staff and church.
Whet people's appetites: "What would it look like if you led five people a year to Christ? How would that change *your* life?"

How to Build Evangelistic Culture

We lead people into full, life-long commitments to Jesus.

> *"In an acceptable time I have heard you,*
> *And in the day of salvation I have helped you."*
> *Behold, now is the accepted time; behold, now is the day of salvation.*
> — *2 Corinthians 6:2*

Part of your responsibility as a senior leader is to introduce your people to God's heart for the lost. If you can incorporate evangelism into the culture of your church, you will be amazed at the results.

1. Be the change you want to see.
If you want to build a culture of evangelism in your church, take steps to make evangelism an active part of your life. Give yourself an easy goal, such as, "I will share my faith with one person a week." That will change your life as a pastor!

2. Make evangelism a priority in your church.
As your church begins to perceive God's love for people, translate that understanding into actual lifestyle priorities. Do you give altar calls at your church? Does your church regularly do outreaches?

3. Create an environment of hospitality for visitors.
Are your services geared to include non-believers? Not everything that happens in a prophetic environment will make

sense to visitors. How will you bridge that barrier? Try to create an environment of hospitality for non-Christians and new Christians in your church.

How to Build Evangelistic Lifestyle

We naturally practice proclamation and power evangelism.

> Then He said to His disciples, "The harvest truly is plentiful, but the laborers are few. Therefore pray the Lord of the harvest to send out laborers into His harvest."
> — Matthew 9:37-38

Out of all the priorities of Heaven, nothing compares to the importance of reaching the lost. One of the few things we *cannot* do after we get to Heaven is reach the lost. As leaders, how can we make evangelism a more prominent expression in our congregations?

1. Have a vision for souls.
What is God's heart for the broken, hurting people around you? Let Him share with you the compassion He feels for them, and then begin to turn the vision of your church toward the harvest.

2. Motivate people with joy.
Tell your church about the responsibility we have as children of God to share our faith—but don't speak from a place of duty. Instead, help people understand the *joy* they can experience when they go out into the harvest (see Luke 15:7).

3. Mix it up.
Help people find creative ways to reach the lost, and celebrate those who are telling others about Jesus, praying for people and walking in prophetic evangelism.

How to Build Evangelistic Structure

We are adding new members through conversion growth.

*For the wages of sin is death, but the gift of God is
eternal life in Christ Jesus our Lord.*
— Romans 6:23

As your church moves into a culture and lifestyle of evangelism,
how can you structure your growth and cause it to increase?

1. Assign an outreach leader to every small group.
An outreach leader helps his small group stay "outwardly
focused." This leader can take simple steps to remind people
about the lost. No matter the reason or focus of the small group,
challenges like this have value and power because they get us
out of our comfort zones.

2. Prepare people to share the gospel...at church.
Make sure your church's main meeting is an evangelistic
expression in some way. Your ushers and prayer ministers need
to know how to share their faith. Take them through a simple
process of how to lead someone to Christ.

3. Set up creative outreaches.
With your leadership team, sit down and come up with different
ways your church could have an impact on your city and region.

4. Be strategic and make friends.
Join community organizations, school boards, sports teams,
Meetup groups and other kinds of groups, and build friendships
among the unreached, showing God's love, and injecting the
gospel when the time is right.

How to Build Evangelistic Leadership

We are effectively training, releasing and mentoring evangelists.

Therefore, having been justified by faith, we have peace with God through our Lord Jesus Christ.
— Romans 5:1

We can't spend much time in the New Testament without realizing it has an urgency for the gospel. John 3:16 isn't a Christian colloquialism or just a verse all of us memorized in Sunday School—it is our lifeblood, our foundation. We carry an incredible message in earthen vessels. Yes, we might feel intimidated at times. Yes, people might reject our message, but those things are very small when compared to the benefits that will flood people's lives as they find what their hearts have been seeking: relationship with God.

The word *evangelist* means a person who brings good news to others. People with this gifting are excellent recruiters and promoters. They are so convinced of the quality of what they have to give that they boldly share it with anyone who will listen and have a hard time giving up until a person comes into agreement with them. They are confident and convinced that everyone should see the world as they do and they are not afraid to tell them so. Who in your congregation consistently shares "good news" with others? Whose heart breaks for the lost?

Preach on the topic of evangelism, see who responds and begin to draw these people aside. Pray with them and start putting together an evangelistic team who will eventually be able to teach classes, lead teams out in the community and instill their love for the lost in other members of your church.

PASTORAL COMMUNITY

We value a loving community of care, counsel and Kingdom culture.

> *The Lord is my shepherd;*
> *I shall not want.*
> *— Psalm 23:1*

At the heart of every pastor is the cultivation of caring community—community that responds in counsel, love and true support for its people. Like an experienced shepherd, the pastor helps feed the people, shelters them as they grow, provides for them and protects them spiritually from harm.

Many places in Scripture talk about what it means to be a pastor. One of the most beautiful and thorough descriptions is found in Psalm 23, where David illustrates how the shepherd functions and how God is the ultimate example of a pastor—the good Shepherd who cares for the flock. In Psalm 23 we see several aspects of the pastoral function. The psalm reveals the heart of God in amazing ways:

- We shall not be in want, which implies there will always be provision.
- God prepares a place for us beside still waters and green pastures.
- He gives us provision, covering and protection.
- He restores our souls.
- He leads us in paths of righteousness.
- He comforts us in death and difficult circumstances.
- He protects us.
- He corrects us.
- He prepares a table before us in the presence of our enemies.
- Goodness and mercy follow us all the days of our lives.
- We will dwell in His house forever.

Another pastoral passage is Ezekiel 34, where the shepherds sinned against the Lord by not taking care of His flock. John 21 is a well-known passage about shepherding, where Jesus talks to Peter about feeding and caring for His sheep.

In summary, the pastoral gift has tremendous power and should never be neglected, despite the current emphasis on the apostolic and creating apostolic resource centers. Even though we are in a massive transition from pastoral to apostolic, we don't ever want to minimize the importance of the pastoral role. It is absolutely essential for every healthy church to have thriving community and relationship between its members. The gift of shepherd in the Body of Christ is extremely essential to the wellbeing of God's people and should never be seen as secondary or somehow less important.

Under apostolic leadership pastors create caring community; a sense of connectivity and mutual interdependency; and a place where care, counsel and concern are cultivated. All members of the Body of Christ need to belong, and it is the pastoral gift that creates that sense of belonging and family in the body.

A Closer Look at Pastoral Care and Small Groups

Pastoring is an essential part of Jesus' ministry in the New Testament, and God describes Himself as a Shepherd multiple times in the Old Testament as well. King David learned to shepherd Israel by shepherding his father's flocks, and in Psalm 23 he describes the pastor's role as a provider, protector, healer, feeder and comforter. According to Ephesians 4:11, pastors exist not only to care for the flock, but they also equip the saints to pastor and care for one another.

Unfortunately, many pastors end up burning out because they try to care for everyone's needs by themselves. The average church in America has only about 60 members (this is often called the "80 Barrier") because that is all one person can pastor. The key to breaking the classic 80 Barrier is delegating pastoral leadership to others. Historically, this was done through assistant pastors and adult Sunday School leaders. In the last 40 years, however, it was accomplished primarily through small groups or cell group ministry. Small groups are essential for many reasons. They provide a place for friendship and fellowship, a context in which growing disciples can minister to one another and a place for Kingdom community to happen. Without small groups, many people end up feeling alienated and isolated, but in small groups, most pastoral needs are met without the direct involvement of the pastoral staff. The individual members of the church provide the love, care, healing and blessing that used to be the domain of a single leader.

Even if we don't consider ourselves pastoral, we can expand our ability in this area by studying the pastoral, learning *how* to pastor others and being around pastoral people. Not every leader in the Body of Christ is called to be a pastor in the fivefold sense or will function with pastoral leadership as his or her primary gift. But that doesn't need to hinder the leader from being pastoral.

How to Build Pastoral Vision

We are a loving community that welcomes and enfolds newcomers.

> *"The thief does not come except to steal, and to kill, and to destroy. I have come that they may have life, and that they may have it more abundantly. I am the good shepherd. The good shepherd gives His life for the sheep."*
> *— John 10:10-11*

As the senior leader, you are the custodian of your church's vision. You are the one who is responsible, as a steward, to be sure the vision of a loving community is continually expressed and modeled by the leaders around you.

1. Connect with God.
Understand God's heart for your church and for each individual within your church. Pay attention to His voice (what He tells you in your personal times with Him), as well as to the prophetic words you receive.

2. Turn to God's Word.
Make a habit of going to the Word of God. Allow your heart to be continually refreshed through Scripture.

3. Write and publicize your vision.
Vision provides a sense of purpose for the pain people go through and the sacrifices they're making. Use outside sources to confirm your vision.

4. Celebrate.
Share on-going testimonies of those who are successfully creating community.

How to Build Pastoral Culture

We foster care and community in every stage and need of life.

> *"I am the good shepherd; and I know My sheep, and am known by My own."*
> *— John 10:14*

God is entirely motivated by love. Love moves His hands to action and is the driving force of His heart. Our freedom is a pulsing desire within Him. Building a pastoral culture in your church will help each member walk in the freedom and love God has made available to us. The Church represents the Good Shepherd on the earth—therefore, true and tender care needs to be a part of our culture.

1. Have a strong value for God's Father-heart.
Building a culture that cares requires we consider the heart of God and have a value for fathering.

2. Infuse that culture into your primary team.
As a leader, give your core team a vision and infuse them with the values and priorities that will help them take the vision as their own and spread it through the congregation.

3. Bring the culture to your congregation.
Culture reflects the senior leader's lifestyle and the core community of the leadership team. Show your church what it looks like to walk in loving community with one another. Begin to instill culture in your congregation through personal interaction, public preaching, testimonies and ongoing celebration of cultural successes.

How to Build Pastoral Lifestyle

We provide excellent support for singles, marriages, families and children.

> *When the Chief Shepherd appears, you will receive the crown of glory that does not fade away.*
> — *1 Peter 5:4*

When you look at the body of believers in your care, do you see the pastoral gift at work among them? The following questions will help paint a picture of the "pastoral state" of your congregation:

- How inclined are the people toward fellowship?
- Do they enjoy just hanging out with one another?
- How much do they want to be together?
- Do they spend time together having fun over a meal, opening up their hearts and homes to one another?

1. Raise up the vision for pastoral care.
Your senior leader and leadership team need to make a conscious effort to model the pastoral gift in everyday settings.

2. Get rid of hindrances.
Begin to identify challenges that might be hindering you and your church from living a pastoral lifestyle. Are your values and priorities consistent with who Jesus is?

3. Consistently share the vision with the body.
Preach on the subject of building a lifestyle of pastoral care in your church, and encourage people to celebrate those who are walking in true, godly love with one another.

How to Build Pastoral Structure

We host small groups where people minister to one another.

> *May the God of peace who brought up our Lord Jesus from the dead, that great Shepherd of the sheep, through the blood of the everlasting covenant, make you complete in every good work to do His will.*
> *— Hebrews 13:20-21*

Jesus is the Good Shepherd. He is the One who supports us, leads us, guides us, feeds us and restores our souls when we are weary and broken, and every church needs to reflect His heart of care and love. Pastoral ministry is woven into every aspect of the church, whether you're a senior leader, parking attendant, janitor, worship leader or children's ministry worker. All of us are involved in caring for one another.

Hospital Ministries
A church is a "hospital" for ill or injured people who need care, "physical therapy" and restoration. The hospital includes your prayer ministries and supportive inner healing and counseling ministries.

Family Ministries
Every church needs ministries that support the family: children's ministry, nursery ministry, youth ministry, premarital counseling,

small group connectivity and other community-building ministries.

Home Groups

Try to have at least 70 percent of Sunday's attendance be involved in small groups. Obviously, this takes work and time to accomplish, but as you put this ministry in place and watch it grow, you will never regret the rewards you receive as a church.

How to Build Pastoral Leadership

We effectively train, release and mentor new pastoral leaders.

> *For you were like sheep going astray, but have now returned to the Shepherd and Overseer of your souls.*
> — 1 Peter 2:25

Who are you raising up? Who is your legacy? Look at your congregation and see which individuals have a pastoral calling. You could also use a gift assessment tool like the one we have at **www.DestinyFinder.com** to help narrow down and identify the gifts and callings of individuals in your church.

As you preach on pastoral care and the shepherd's heart, from time to time do "altar calls" for those who believe they are called to pastoral ministry. Begin to note who those individuals are, and gather them together periodically and pour into them. Put them in positions of leadership that will highlight their gifting so they can be more impactful. Give them permission to function pastorally in their small groups and other ministry groups they may be involved in.

Help people discover themselves as caregivers. There are people in your congregation who may be more "people oriented" than you, and they can be trained as connectors who create a sense of love, care and community in the church. Foster that kind of relationship with your team.

TEACHING TRANSFORMATION

We value the power of truth that brings teaching, training and transformation.

> *Oh, how I love Your law!*
> *It is my meditation all the day.*
> — *Psalm 119:97*

From the books of Moses through the Psalms, the life of Jesus and the epistles, it is clear that loving the Word of the Lord is a key to knowing and walking with Him.

In standard charismatic teaching, two distinct words describe the way God speaks. *Logos* usually refers to the eternal, firm Word of God; it is our plumb line and point of reference. *Rhema* normally refers to the momentary word of the Lord—that is, it is the word God speaks prophetically through the "still, small voice" within or through the use of spiritual gifts. The prophetic word of the Lord must never contradict the written Word of the Lord. The gift and ministry of the teacher are absolutely essential to upholding Scripture (*logos*) as we continue to grow in the gift and ministry of prophecy (*rhema*).

Teachers are entrusted with the Word of God at a special level. Jesus was called the Great Teacher. Paul, who was truly a teacher's teacher, laid out the aspects of redemption with a beautiful and precise perfection. Look at the way he handled questions of salvation in the book of Romans, or the nature of the Church and of the believer's identity in Ephesians. His teachings are profoundly insightful and a model for every teacher.

Teaching is not merely the articulation of ideas and principles, but it is a supernatural activity by which an anointed teacher can bring words of affirmation to the human heart. A person gifted in teaching has the God-given ability to take truth, break it into bite-sized pieces and deliver it to the very point of the human heart where confusion and deception have occurred. The teacher can release the truth that displaces the lie and bring the hearer into the freedom Jesus described when He said, "The truth shall make you free." (Note the condition in the preceeding verse, which is actually the first part of the sentence: "If you continue in my word then you are truly my disciples and you will know the truth and the truth shall make you free." John 8:31-32) Just as the evangelist is centered on the good news and salvation of the lost, and the pastor is centered on love and community, the teacher is centered on truth and the power of truth to bring transformation.

The keys to the teacher's heart are communicating and conveying truth for training and transformation. Different gifts are at work in the Body of Christ, and unfortunately, in prophetic movements the teacher gift can end up being disregarded. It was the predominant gift in the Body of Christ prior to this time; those who could declare sound doctrine were considered the pinnacle of leadership. However, this led the Body of Christ to focus more on the letter of the law, not life in the Spirit.

Thankfully, the majority of us have come out of that, but we need to be careful we don't correct too far. As Jesus said, truth sets us free. It isn't the truth we *hear* that makes us free; it is the truth that confronts falsehood inside us—truth that deals with the lies and evicts them from our hearts. That is the truth that actually has value. This requires an anointed teacher, who can bring truth to the human heart.

Even if we don't consider ourselves to be teachers, we can expand our ability to teach by studying the teaching gift, learning *how* to be teachers and being around people who are gifted in this area.

How to Build Teaching Vision

Our members are biblically literate and theologically informed.

> *But his delight is in the law of the Lord,*
> *And in His law he meditates day and night.*
> — *Psalm 1:2*

The Bible is our hub, mandate and launching point; it is our constitution in the Kingdom of Heaven. The Scriptures are our full and final authority on true faith and practice. All of us need to wrap our hearts around the Word of God and be transformed by His awesome truth.

1. Celebrate the vision.
As a leader, have a vision that will cause people to understand the power of the Word and bring them into right alignment with it. Vision for the Word needs to be celebrated again and again.

2. Show people what the vision looks like.
Incorporate love for the Word deeply into your own life, and actively seek ways you and your team could fall more in love with God's Word.

3. Inspire people and make the vision a priority.
Spend time preaching about God's Word and study it as a congregation, equipping your church to really delve into its truth. Celebrate the Word in personal areas of independent study, meditation and memorization. Inspire people and show them how powerful the Word of God can be in daily life.

How to Build Teaching Culture

Our members value Scripture study on an individual and corporate level.

> *For the word of God is living and powerful, and sharper than any two-edged sword, piercing even to the division of soul and spirit, and of joints and marrow, and is a discerner of the thoughts and intents of the heart.*
> *— Hebrews 4:12*

The teacher has a powerful love for God's Word that can spread through your entire church. As you build a culture around love for the Word, God's truth will become a firm, established part of your congregation.

1. Make the culture a part of your life.
Culture reflects the senior leader's lifestyle and the core community of the leadership team. How has the Word impacted you? Does your family study the Word together on a regular basis?

2. Make the culture a foundational aspect of your primary **team.**
Build a culture that honors Scripture. What are the values that illustrate integrity, consistency and intelligence in the Kingdom of God?

3. Build the culture in your congregation.
Through personal interaction, public preaching, testimonies and ongoing celebration of cultural successes, begin to build in your congregation a culture that loves God's Word.

How to Build Teaching Lifestyle

We provide intensive, personal discipleship for new and growing believers.

> Great peace have those who love Your law,
> And nothing causes them to stumble.
> — Psalm 119:165

Teachers are knowledgeable people who seek to understand facts. They care deeply about the truth and comprehend the power of truth to set people free and help them thrive. Love for the Word of God courses through their veins—they make passionate educators—and gifted teachers are usually the ones who teach Bible and lifestyle classes within the church and provide detailed training. Along the way, they impart their gift and love for the Word into others.

1. Remind people of the vision.
As leaders, we get to reveal God's heart as we encourage those around us to go deep into God's Word and to teach others to do the same. Lives are changed as a lifestyle of loving the Word is embraced and established in a church.

2. Make God's Word a priority.
Does anything hinder your church from living a lifestyle of passion for Scripture and the truth of God?

3. Get people excited.
People need to make Scripture a part of them and explore its pages to truly understand and experience it. The Word will come alive in their hearts and they will "feast" on Scripture in a way that excites and inspires them to share it with others.

How to Build Teaching Structure

Every member is equipped to equip others with the truth of Scripture.

> If you really fulfill the royal law according to the Scripture, "You shall love your neighbor as yourself," you do well.
> — James 2:8

How do you train people in the Word of God? Let's look at a few hands-on, practical ways you can help grow a deep love for God's Word in your congregation.

1. Have adult classes that teach the Word.
Though most transformation doesn't take place in a classroom, the necessary *fuel* for transformation can.

2. Help people own what they learn.
What they are learning needs to take root inside them and be carried out the door with them when they leave each day.

3. Have leaders train up leaders and encourage small groups.
In every ministry, group or class, your leaders need to train up their replacements. Make sure your people are invested in small groups, communicating with each other and processing Scripture together as a normal part of their Christian life/community experience.

4. Make sure you're doing it first.
Build structures that begin in the heart and grow out from the center. Make the love and study of Scripture a priority in your own life, and then try to build it in the lives of the next generation of leaders, so they in turn can do it with other people in your church.

How to Build Teaching Leadership

We effectively train, release and mentor new gifted teachers.

> Your word is very pure;
> Therefore Your servant loves it.
> — Psalm 119:140

Do you know who the gifted teachers are in your church? What can you do to engage with them and promote the love for God's Word among your people?

Unfortunately, teachers don't always survive well in prophetic environments because they love the Word of God so much and can become offended if Scripture seems to be undervalued. We encourage you to look for those teachers. Celebrate them and pull them up to a new level of participation. Get them engaged and train them. Bible schools and seminaries exist primarily for those who are called to teach; they train teachers. Obviously, not every teacher has to go to seminary, but we recommend those who are called to teach consider it because of the strong foundations these schools can lay in the teacher's gift and spiritual abilities.

As you build within your church community a passion for the Word of God, you will be amazed at the changes that occur in your congregation. Celebrate the actual teachers in your midst (those in the office of teacher), as well as the "ordinary" members of the church who love God's Word and are sharing His truths with others.

KINGDOM ADMINISTRATION

We value administrative excellence in managing ministry and mission.

> *His divine power has granted to us everything pertaining to life and godliness, through the true knowledge of Him who called us by His own glory and excellence.*
> — *2 Peter 1:3 (NASB)*

A gift of the Spirit, administration is an important and powerful part of Kingdom reality. It is spoken of in 1 Corinthians 12:28 and Romans 12:7-8, and administrators had high value throughout Scripture. They were people who could coordinate, mobilize and move things forward for the nation of Israel and the Body of Christ as a whole.

Those who manage the logistics and tactics of an army are vital, and unfortunately, many churches have experienced various kinds of failures because of poor administration and the unwise allocation of resources. Administrators steer entire groups toward a goal and allow resources to be channeled in such a way that maximum impact is achieved.

Jesus depended on administrators while He walked the earth. Certain women traveled with Him and helped administrate His group in practical, logistical ways (see Luke 8). Later in the book of Acts, Greek widows were not being served well, and the apostles realized the need for administrators, so in Acts 6 they set aside servants who helped administrate practical matters. The word *deacon* isn't used in Acts 6, but this event with the Greek widows was the emergence of the deaconal role.

Deacons and Elders

Many churches don't use the word *deacon* anymore, but in the local church structure of the New Testament, elder and deacon were the two primary job descriptions. The elder is called to pastor and oversee *people*, while the deacon oversees projects and functions. *Diakonos,* which we translate as "deacon," means the ability to serve and administrate on someone else's behalf— it is the person who is good with numbers, details and keeping an organization running smoothly.

The realm of the administrator is vast and significant, because every gift has an administrative dimension. Pastors, evangelists, prophets, teachers and apostles need to mobilize others and send people to do certain tasks. They need help writing budgets; allocating resources of time, energy and money; keeping calendars and schedules; and a host of other details. Some people look at everything that needs to be done and panic—but administrators are gifted in seeing the details and orchestrating them in a way that lets the ship sail forward smoothly.

In essence, the realm of the administrator is the ministry of excellence working within the quality of how we manage our resources and accomplish our goals in the most effective, efficient way.

What Lies Ahead

Not only do administrators help a church with its present needs, but they are also able to look into the future. They see the steps that need to be taken so the end goal can be reached, and they plan accordingly.

God has called us to go out and change the world. This requires us to move beyond just managing what we have *right now* and begin to perceive what lies ahead. We can marshal our resources for future management. Strategic planning is a process of investigating the present (understanding what we are doing in the here and now) and mapping the journey into the future. It is the ability to mobilize human resources, financial resources and calendar and organizational resources in such a way that we accomplish all God has directed us to accomplish.

A Note on Administration and Kingdom Strategy

Administration and strategic planning are similar gifts, but they are different enough that we included them as separate themes in this assessment. Administration (theme six) is the management of resources, projects, facilities and finances that facilitate the church's ministries and care for its members. On the other hand, Kingdom strategy (theme seven) is more futuristic. It sees where the church or ministry is *going* versus where it is right now. You could say that administration is management, while strategic planning is projection.

As you go through this theme, keep in mind your finances, facilities, calendar, media and Internet. Are the following statements true of your church?

- We encourage and practice wise and faith-filled financial stewardship.
- Our facilities are functional and well suited to fulfill our mission and vision.
- We manage our calendar effectively in light of our purpose and priorities.
- We effectively share our message through various forms of media.
- Our website is creative, accurate, comprehensive, current and well used.

How to Build an Administrative Vision of Excellence

We promote a vision for excellence in the church.

> *And He is before all things, and in Him all things consist.*
> — *Colossians 1:17*

God is an administrator. He runs a universe of a hundred billion planets and He's good at it. There is order and structure, growth and purpose. Organizational excellence depends on wise administration and strategic planning. Simply stated, the vision for administration is excellence in everything we do. We are a people of high quality who reflect the excellence of our Father and the Kingdom of Heaven. The quality of our work and lives should be in a continual process of improvement because we are moving from "glory to glory" even in practical matters.

1. Talk about excellence.
Show the church why you love excellence, how it has affected your life and how it can change theirs. Every aspect of ministry should reflect your administrative value for excellence, effectiveness and efficiency of use.

2. Make your vision for excellence a priority for your staff and church.
Celebrate excellence in your core leadership group in such a way that your vision for excellence extends to the rest of the church.

3. Demonstrate excellence: Be an excellent steward.
How are you giving back to your community? How are you blessing and being generous with your neighbors, even those who don't attend your church or don't agree with you?

How to Build a Culture of Administrative Excellence

Our culture supports development and growth from "glory to glory."

> *"His lord said to him, 'Well done, good and faithful servant; you were faithful over a few things, I will make you ruler over many things. Enter into the joy of your lord.'"*
> *— Matthew 25:21*

It isn't necessary for prophetic cultures to "shoot from the hip," so to speak. We can be prophetic *and* good stewards of our time, energy and talents. We can be prophetic *and* produce excellent material, products and resources that benefit the people we are trying to reach.

1. Be the change you want to see.
Determine the values that promote excellence, such as the glory of God (that which clearly reveals Him) and generosity (where stewardship and relational integrity are clearly modeled). Is the desire to help people walk in excellence integrated into your values, priorities and practices as a leader?

2. Share the change.
As a leader, give your people a vision and infuse them with the values and priorities that will help them become promoters of excellence in their own right.

3. Publish the change.
Proof all your church publications for errors. Keep superb records and inspire your people to do the same. Try to consider excellence in practical ways.

How to Build Administrative Lifestyle

We live in a way that doesn't overextend our resources.

> *"My Lord, if I have now found favor in Your sight, do not pass on by Your servant."*
> — *Genesis 18:3*

Just as God is excellent in everything He does, we should have a value for excellence in everything we do on a practical level. We can strive to help our members become excellent stewards in every respect. Living a lifestyle of excellence on a personal level encompasses a person's resources, destiny, careful management of finances, avoidance of debt and so forth.

1. Model excellence for your church.
We want to model the character and nature of our Father every
opportunity we get. Pursuing excellence is one of the ways we
do this because He has called us by His own excellence (2 Peter
1:3).

2. Get rid of obstacles.
What stands between your church and a high level of excellence
in everything you do?

3. Encourage excellence in others' lives.
Incorporate the pursuit of excellence deeply into your own life—
take the time to do things well. Go before God and ask Him to
show you what excellence looks like in your personal life.
Encourage excellence in every context, whether it is in people's
homes, home groups, Sunday morning services, workplaces,
governmental spheres or even at the gym.

How to Build Administrative Structure

We uncover what we need and work together for growth.

> Do you not know that those who run in a race all run, but
> one receives the prize? Run in such a way that you may
> obtain it.
> — 1 Corinthians 9:24

In your congregation, do you have ministries available that assist
both the individual and the church corporately in the
administration of excellence? What do these ministries look like?

1. Determine what people need and offer training.
Offer adult classes that focus on issues like finances and time
and destiny management. Query the congregation; find out the
areas they feel they need to grow in and then make those
classes available. Build relationships on purpose, asking, "How
can I serve you? What can I do to help you grow?"

2. Seek to sow excellence into your structures.

Build the spirit of excellence into the structures that support your church: media, music, sound systems, lighting, computer programs, applications, etc.

3. Raise up administrators.

Raise up people with the gift of true administration in their lives. Address administration, both its importance and its calling, from the pulpit and see who responds. Create entry-level admin roles, where people can demonstrate faithfulness without a tremendous amount of expertise, and midlevel administrative roles, which help them grow. Equip those who are uniquely called to administration, and help them raise up administrative sons and daughters.

How to Build Administrative Leadership

We effectively train, release and mentor new gifted administrators.

> *Therefore we also, since we are surrounded by so great a cloud of witnesses, let us lay aside every weight, and the sin which so easily ensnares us, and let us run with endurance the race that is set before us.*
> *— Hebrews 12:1*

The Bible clearly says that we represent God on the earth (2 Corinthians 5:20). Who in your church takes that understanding seriously? Who walks in excellence in her job and how she serves other people? Who has revealed an aptitude for details and order?

Identify these people and begin to speak to them about their gifts and potential for service. Meet with them regularly and build a team of administrators who are capable, talented and intent on serving God with excellence.

Encourage excellence in every context, whether it is in people's homes, home groups, Sunday morning services, workplaces, governmental spheres or even at the gym.

KINGDOM STRATEGY

We value supernatural strategic planning in bringing God's purpose to pass.

The Lord was with Joseph, and he was a successful man; and he was in the house of his master the Egyptian. And his master saw that the Lord was with him and that the Lord made all he did to prosper in his hand.
— Genesis 39:2-3

In many ways, the story God is writing in your life is a mystery. He is God, which means He is able to do exceedingly abundantly above all we ask or think, and He is able to accomplish these things in a sequence all His own. This means there will be seasons when things fall into place without your help. It will seem like everything is working out on its own. You will look around and realize that God is arranging the story and moving the pieces as He sees fit. In these seasons, it is apparent that He has an agenda and timeline, and He is in the mood to get things done.

But that is just a season. It doesn't always work that way.

God gave us logical minds and the ability to extrapolate, plan, set things in order and walk out goals and conditions. Scripture tells us to run our races well:

Do you not know that those who run in a race all run, but one receives the prize? Run in such a way that you may obtain it.
— 1 Corinthians 9:24

Let us run with endurance the race that is set before us.
— Hebrews 12:1

Apart from God *commandeering* our efforts and taking us in a vastly different direction, it is always wise to have a plan with goals and objectives in mind. Unfortunately, one reason the Church has been limited in its effectiveness is our frequent inability to set clear goals and achieve those goals within intended timeframes.

The Difference Between Goals and Objectives

Goals are large outcomes—the end result, the distant target. Objectives, meanwhile, are sub-goals that allow you to achieve outcomes in a carefully executed manner. In football terms, the primary "goal" is winning the game. The objectives are a series of points scored through touchdowns and field goals.

Corporately speaking, many goals and objectives are practical considerations: "What kind of resources do we need? How much money? What kind of facility?" Obtaining those resources could be a set of objectives. Another set of objectives is uncovered as we answer these questions: "What kind of team do we need to accomplish our goal? How long will it take to build that team, and how are we going to build it? What are the different steps and stages of building?"

Each of your goals needs to be broken down into large-to-small sequences that can be prioritized and implemented. If your vision is to secure a building, for example, a set of reasonable factors comes into play: First, you need to start looking for a building and contract a realtor. You need to figure out the necessary square footage and how much money you have available to finish out the building. Those are reasonable steps that enable you to move forward.

Define the things you want to accomplish: Win the game. Lead at halftime. Have great team dynamics. Grow the church. Raise up leaders. Reach the lost. Pay the bills. Once you understand where you're going and the commitment it will take to get there, it becomes relatively simple to set things in order.

The Kingdom Plan

Every prophetic environment has five general Kingdom goals:

1. Receive vision from the Lord and communicate it to your congregation.
2. Build the vision, your leaders and your congregations.
3. Reach the lost.
4. Create connection and community.
5. Communicate truth in a transformational way.

Those are our primary goals, and from these goals, each church builds a set of objectives that are more specific to its calling and region.

How to Build Kingdom Strategy Vision

We regularly and prayerfully plan and execute according to God's purpose.

> Now to Him who is able to do exceedingly abundantly above all that we ask or think, according to the power that works in us, to Him be glory in the church by Christ Jesus to all generations, forever and ever. Amen.
> — Ephesians 3:20-21

God likes to plan. He sees the end from the beginning and works all things according to the counsel of His will (Ephesians 1:11). He is outside of time—interacting with all time, at the same time, in His eternal timeframe. Therefore, He is able to move us forward with a degree of intention and yet still allow us to be free moral agents who are able to participate or not participate according to our willingness to choose His grace. Just as He is a strategic thinker, we are called to be strategic thinkers.

1. Seek God for His vision.
On a regular basis, come before God and pray, "Okay, Father. What is Your heart? How can we more effectively align our church with what matters to You?"

2. Keep the vision in front of the people.
Consistently give your people a fresh sense of God's purpose for the church.

3. Make sure your values and priorities match your vision.
Direct your time, energy and various ministries toward what God has told you to do.
7.3

How to Build Kingdom Strategy Culture

We regularly review why we exist and what we must do to fulfill our ministry.

> *For I know the thoughts that I think toward you, says the Lord, thoughts of peace and not of evil, to give you a future and a hope.*
> — *Jeremiah 29:11*

Jesus had a very specific target group when He was on the earth. He declared, "I didn't come for everyone—I came for the lost sheep of Israel." Obviously, in His plan for the rest of the world God knew He would be sending Paul to the nations a few years later, but Jesus' primary target was clear, and for the most part, He remained focused on that target. Just as He did with Jesus, God has a target for each of us.

1. What is your target?
As a church, define your target and know who you are called to reach. This makes things simpler for you: "This is who we are. This is who we're called to reach. They are our target—and then beyond them, we can reach and serve other people as well."

2. Know your team in light of your target.
Not every team member needs to be exactly like the people you're reaching, but cross-cultural ministry requires you to be more intentional in the process than you would have to be otherwise.

3. Understand your values and priorities.
Be sure your priorities match your vision, because your actions as a church prove what is really important to you.

How to Build Kingdom Strategy Lifestyle

Our ministry goals are defined, measurable and attainable.

> But He said to them, "I must preach the kingdom of God to the other cities also, because for this purpose I have been sent."
> — Luke 4:43

God is a purposeful Being. He has a plan, and He encourages us to plan according to His plan, remembering we are completely dependent upon Him. We need to work in partnership with Him to accomplish the purposes He ordained for us. A *vision* is what you see. A *mission* is what you do to accomplish what you see, and a mission without goals is just an idea. All our goals and objectives need to be placed before the Lord, with a sense of dependence upon Him.

1. Make your goals well defined.
Goals need to be friendly, inclusive, fun—and rational, too. What are you going after? What is your specific outcome? How do you define this intended outcome in terms of quality and magnitude?

2. Make your goals measurable.
How many people are developing into maturity? How many leaders are taking on new leadership in your church?

3. Make your goals attainable.

Momentum is a factor of many little successes, and those little successes will work to increase your velocity, so your church can accomplish the bigger things God has for you.

How to Build Kingdom Strategy Structure

Our ministry structures are flexible, effective and life giving.

> *So it was, from the time that he had made him overseer of his house and all that he had, that the Lord blessed the Egyptian's house for Joseph's sake; and the blessing of the Lord was on all that he had in the house and in the field.*
> — *Genesis 39:5*

God has invited you to partner with Him, fulfilling His intention for your city and the people He has given you to lead. When you know His intentions and overall plan, you can build structures (programs and ministries within your church) that are consistent with His plan and are also effective in terms of reaching the people around you. Your people especially need these structures because they aren't exposed to the vision as much as you are. As the leader, you know the plan well because you're around it 24 hours a day, but your average member is getting only two to three hours of exposure to you a week. With the right structures in place, you can lead people more effectively.

1. Make your structures intentional.
Your programs and ministries need to match your purpose as a church.

2. Make your structures goal oriented.
Build a culture of intentionality in your church, so people know what they want to achieve and when.

3. Make your structures life giving.
Programs should be servants to the people who are carrying them.

How to Build Kingdom Strategy Leadership

Our team is cohesive, united and suited to our ministry target group.

The keeper of the prison did not look into anything that was under Joseph's authority, because the Lord was with him; and whatever he did, the Lord made it prosper.
— *Genesis 39:23*

God's Word says that the horse is prepared for battle, but the victory is the Lord's. In other words, we do our part and God does His. The book of Proverbs speaks again and again about the power of planning and wise counsel. Strategically minded people are like weapons in the hand of a general. Theory alone won't get us far—we need strategy and structure to carry us toward our goals.

When you look at the people in your church, who has a gift and talent for strategic planning? Who knows how to set goals and accomplish them with a specific timeframe? When you speak about the importance of strategy and how God uses our plans, who in the church responds? Draw these people aside and begin to minister to them specifically. Put them in positions of leadership in the church so their gifts and callings can be more clearly seen.

As you begin to think more intentionally about your team and strategize with God about His plans, He will give you an ever-increasing, thriving church that will be able to bring transformation to the region around you.

KINGDOM SERVANTHOOD

We value biblical servanthood as an expression of Kingdom ministry.

God considers Himself a servant. It is a shocking concept when you think about it at length. He is the Creator of all things...and yet servanthood is a deep, intimate part of His heart. Jesus reiterated this idea again and again:

> *"He who is greatest among you shall be your servant."*
> — *Matthew 23:11*

> *"Blessed are those servants whom the master, when he comes, will find watching. Assuredly, I say to you that he will gird himself and have them sit down to eat, and will come and serve them."*
> — *Luke 12:37*

When we demonstrate Jesus in practical ways by serving other people, not only do we make a difference in people's immediate lives, but we also gain the right to lead them. The world will listen to a person who is a true servant.

In John 13 when Jesus was with His friends in the upper room, He humbled Himself and washed their feet. Scripture indicates that His ability to model servanthood was based in His absolute security in His identity. Jesus knew "that the Father had given all things into His hands, and that He had come from God and was going to God" (verse 3). Later in verse 14 He said, "If I then, your Lord and Teacher, have washed your feet, you also ought to wash one another's feet." Servanthood is the foundation for all leadership and influence. Servanthood and leadership are two sides of the same coin. As Bill Johnson, senior leader of Bethel Church in Redding, California, says, "Rule with the heart of a servant. Serve with the heart of a king."

Paul also made the servant heart of God very clear:

> Let this mind be in you which was also in Christ
> Jesus, who, being in the form of God, did not consider it
> robbery to be equal with God, but made Himself of no
> reputation, taking the form of a bondservant, and coming
> in the likeness of men.
> — Philippians 2:6-7

Jesus emptied Himself to be a servant. He is a servant God.
Servanthood is the basis of all true leadership.

Different Types and Times of Servanthood

Administration and deaconal ministry are two different things.
Administration involves looking after resources, the calendar,
facility, finances and technical and media issues. *Deaconal*
ministry, on the other hand, refers to the various servant aspects
of the church—anything that falls within the practical care of its
members: greeting and ushering, running a coffee house or
bookstore and any other ministry that provides services for the
people. Deaconal ministry is sometimes called *non-people
ministry* because it oversees people's practical needs.

Remember that the first time we see deaconal leaders in
Scripture is Luke 8, when women accompanied Jesus and saw
to His practical needs. Later in the book of Acts, deaconal
ministry becomes much clearer. Widows were being neglected in
the distribution of food, and the apostles were asked to address
the issue. They replied, "Choose seven men full of the Holy Spirit
and let them take care of it." The apostles laid hands on these
men and ratified their role. It is interesting that several of the
"deacons" in this context eventually ended up moving into other
powerful ministries. One became an evangelist. Because of the
defense he gave just before his death, some people believe
Stephen became a prophet.

The point is that some people are called to serve the church long term and become senior deacons or workers in the Body of Christ. Others, meanwhile, are called to serve as deacons only for a season as they develop into their full ministry.

Unfortunately, many people serve out of duty when there's a higher motivation: *delight*. Though honorable, duty isn't a sustainable long-term motivator—but if you can find the pleasure of God in the midst of serving others, you can go on to transform the world.

How to Build Servant Vision

Every member of our church embraces the call to serve others.

> *Let a man so consider us, as servants of Christ and stewards of the mysteries of God.*
> *— 1 Corinthians 4:1*

Servanthood should be the heart that drives us as we go out to change the world. We see the good that ought to be done, and we activate ourselves to serve with hearts of genuine love and compassion. Unfortunately, the Church has built a reputation for having the opposite spirit. Some of us haven't served in humility and gentleness; instead, we rode in like bosses and tried to rule people and legislate morality over them. The Church has lost the right to lead because we have lost the will to serve. Until we are willing to serve the poor and ungodly, the just and the unjust— we have no right to expect to be heard. Servanthood opens the door to leadership.

1. Give people practical ways to serve.
The vision to serve comes from the heart of God. If we want to be leaders in the world, we need to be the servants of all (Mark 9:35).

2. Show people what service looks like.
Discover the delight aspect of serving others and then spread
that delight to your leadership team.

3. Make servanthood a foundational aspect of your leadership.
Celebrate servanthood in your core leadership group in such a
way that your vision for servanthood naturally extends to the rest
of the church.

How to Build Servant Culture

Our church provides many and varied service opportunities.

> *The Lord redeems the soul of His servants,*
> *And none of those who trust in Him shall be condemned.*
> *— Psalm 34:22*

All ministry boils down to servanthood with a servant's heart.
That heart did not begin in us—it began in Jesus, who is the
ultimate servant leader. Our goal as servant leaders is to create
a whole congregation of servant leaders who fulfill God's
purposes on the earth.

1. Show people the culture you want them to have.
Model the lifestyle you want to create, and then provide ongoing
opportunities for people to serve. Let the congregation see their
leaders being servants—picking up the paper in the hallway,
cleaning bathrooms, taking meals to sick people, etc.

2. Make that culture part of your primary team.
The leadership team (the senior pastor, spouse and core team
members) needs to model what true service looks like. Preach
about servanthood and talk about how we serve the Lord and
one another through our generosity, sacrifice and willingness to
commit to others.

3. Train your people to dedicate concentrated time to God.
Serving Jesus doesn't always look like going to church meetings or doing street ministry. It can also look like having lunch with a friend who has questions about God or praying with Christian coworkers before starting your workday. Teach people to reach out to others in creative ways.

How to Build a Lifestyle of Servanthood

Our members serve each other in times of crisis and need.

> Let them say continually,
> "Let the Lord be magnified,
> Who has pleasure in the prosperity of His servant."
> — Psalm 35:27

The values you embrace as a church gradually become a way of life for you. If you make servanthood a deep, foundational value in your church, you will see a set of practices begin to emerge in your church that reflects the things your church does naturally. The people do these things because they are entrenched in their hearts as a community. At its core, true servanthood means having a heart that mirrors God's heart. We love and serve one another because He does. Jesus said, "It is enough for a disciple that he be like his teacher, and a servant like his master" (Matthew 10:25).

1. Show people your vision for servanthood.
Make servanthood personal. Incorporate it deeply into your own life, and build it into your family's lifestyle.

2. Prove your values with your priorities.
As a leader, you "prove" the values of your church with your priorities (the way in which you allocate time, energy, money and talent to what you value). What do you truly value?

3. Share your heart for servanthood with the church.
Preach on building a lifestyle of servanthood, and encourage
people to celebrate those who are trying to live as Jesus would—
with servant hearts.

8.5

How to Build Servant Structure

We provide care and support systems for those who serve.

> *Let Your work appear to Your servants,*
> *And Your glory to their children.*
> — *Psalm 90:16*

If Jesus Himself came as a servant (Philippians 2:7), then the
"greatest" among us will be what He said: the servants of all. We
never reach a spiritual level where we are no longer called to
serve. How do you build servant ministries within your church?

1. Model servanthood for the church.
Make the servant heart visible on multiple levels within the
church, from the core outward. The congregation needs to see
its leaders being servants. When the church sees how much you
value servanthood, it will open their hearts to respond in a similar
manner.

2. Raise up servant leaders.
To some extent, building servant ministries depends on the
servant leaders you are raising up—men and women who have
the gift of servanthood evident in their spiritual gift-mix. Put out
calls to serve and see who responds. Identify these people and
put together a core servant (deaconal) team.

3. Train your servant leaders to raise up teams of servants.
In the concentric model of church leadership, people can grow in
the servant calling. They can move from being just helpers who
provide regular support to being part of a servant team. They can

eventually become servant overseers—head workers or deacons who oversee four or five servant ministries.

How to Build Servant Leadership

We recognize servant leaders and release them into new levels of service.

> *Your servant meditates on Your statutes.*
> *— Psalm 119:23*

A true servant's heart loves people and displays mercy. People gifted in servanthood usually are able to connect well with others; they are executors who know how to make decisions, and within their spiritual gift-mix (Romans 12), they are motivated by mercy, giving and serving. A tremendous opportunity exists for the servant or deaconal office to be awakened in the Body of Christ. The more we emphasize it and raise up leaders, the more fruit we will see.

Who is wired to serve in your church? Who expresses the love of God through tangible actions meant to benefit others? When you preach on servanthood, who in the congregation is stirred?

Pull these people aside and begin to give to them as they have given to others. Pour into them and minister to them. Raise them up as servant leaders in your church, and give them the means and opportunity to raise up others.

HEALING MINISTRY

We value healing and deliverance as an expression of God's purpose.

> *"The Spirit of the Lord God is upon Me,*
> *Because the Lord has anointed Me*
> *To preach good tidings to the poor;*
> *He has sent Me to heal the brokenhearted,*
> *To proclaim liberty to the captives,*
> *And the opening of the prison to those who are bound;*
> *To proclaim the acceptable year of the Lord."*
> *— Isaiah 61:1-2*

Isaiah 61 holds an amazing Messianic prophecy that Jesus, the fulfillment of the prophecy, declared at the beginning of His ministry. When He presented His ministry in Nazareth, He read the passage and told His listeners, "This day, this Scripture is fulfilled in your hearing."

What was the core message of this prophecy? That God loves the broken. Isaiah 61 is a key description of *His* ministry to the Church, His beloved bride. As His representatives, we need to be as concerned about people's hearts as He is and equip ourselves to care for and help lead the broken into ever-increasing healing and restoration.

God the Comforter

The world may be in rough shape today, but it didn't start out that way. In the beginning, God declared that His creation was "good." After He created humanity, those made in His image, He even said, "It is very good."

Brokenness came to our planet as a result of sin. The enemy's work released a terrible legacy of sin and brokenness in people's lives, and the vision for healing is embedded in the very heart of God.

As we grow to become more and more like Jesus, we naturally grow into His vision for healing as well. It becomes rooted in our hearts. Healing is the gifts of mercy and compassion at work. Paul wrote in 2 Corinthians 1:3-4, "Blessed be the God and Father of our Lord Jesus Christ, the Father of mercies and God of all comfort, who comforts us in all our tribulation." That is where healing begins—in the comforting process. We are comforted by the One who made us, and as that happens, we are equipped to comfort others with the comfort we received from God.

Every church needs to offer some type of healing ministry and seek to impact people at greater and greater levels in a holistic way, helping them overcome the challenges of life and move forward. The goal is to provide a way for the broken and hurting to encounter God's healing and comfort, so they find relief and restoration in their lives. Healing ministries commonly found in prophetic environments include healing rooms (where teams of people pray for the sick for physical healing), inner healing and professional counseling services.

> *"Comfort, yes, comfort My people!"*
> *Says your God.*
> *"Speak comfort to Jerusalem, and cry out to her,*
> *That her warfare is ended,*
> *That her iniquity is pardoned."*
> — *Isaiah 40:1-2*

How to Build Healing Ministry Vision

We provide specialty small groups with various healing emphases.

> *He will feed His flock like a shepherd;*
> *He will gather the lambs with His arm,*
> *And carry them in His bosom,*
> *And gently lead those who are with young.*
> — *Isaiah 40:11*

God is a Father and Shepherd, and it is His kindness that leads us to repentance (Romans 2:4). David even wrote, "Your right hand has held me up, Your gentleness has made me great" (Psalm 18:35). How can you promote a vision for love and healing in your congregation, so people develop a passion for the healing and comfort of God?

1. Introduce people to their Father.
Comfort is a critical part of any vision for healing, and people need to be in right relationship with their heavenly Father.

2. Help people see their own hearts.
When necessary, gently challenge what people are thinking. In love, correct them when they are mistaken and show them how they can learn to think more wisely, based on the truth of Scripture.

3. Remember your authority in Christ.
Take steps to recognize and learn the authority you have, so you can do what Jesus did.

4. Make healing a priority to your leadership team and church.
In order to make healing a deep, core value in your congregation, it first needs to be a deep, core value to you and your leadership team.

How to Build Healing Ministry Culture

We train peer counselors and provide inner healing for the brokenhearted.

> And behold, a leper came and worshiped Him, saying, "Lord, if You are willing, You can make me clean." Then Jesus put out His hand and touched him, saying, "I am willing; be cleansed." Immediately his leprosy was cleansed.
> — Matthew 8:2-3

The recorded words of Jesus are important, and yet He did more than speak. When we talk about His *words*, we also need to talk about His *works*, because the two go together. The words and works of Jesus form the gospel—they are the good news. He used healing and words of knowledge again and again; the apostles did the same throughout the book of Acts. We need to build in our churches a culture that thrives on both the raw words of the gospel as well as the power of the Lord found in healing.

1. Exemplify the culture you want to build.
A culture of healing offers grace, transformation and trust that honors confidentiality and doesn't penalize its members for their less-than-perfect moments.

2. Make mercy available.
In every meeting, pray for the sick and wounded.

3. Infuse your vision into your primary team and church.
Promote your vision of healing, and equip your church to impact the world around them. Celebrate every healing that occurs.

How to Build Healing Ministry Lifestyle

We provide trained ministers to pray for physical healing.
> *"A bruised reed He will not break,*
> *And smoking flax He will not quench."*
> *— Isaiah 42:3*

What does it mean to live a lifestyle of healing? In simple terms, it means we connect with the heartbeat of God, who loves the broken and downtrodden; He isn't even willing to damage a bruised reed. Mercy and healing can be embedded in a church to such an extent that the people of God become known as people of love.

1. Promote your value for healing.
A lifestyle of healing means we have a consistent value for healing that is visible everywhere within the church, from the

core leadership team to the youngest child attending Sunday school. Essentially, living a lifestyle of healing means we know how to love well.

2. Identify and remove challenges.
After examining your values and priorities, does anything need to be adjusted in your life or church?

3. Share your vision for healing with the body.
Give people the opportunity to learn about healing and develop the necessary skills to live out healing as a lifestyle reality. You can begin to do this by preaching about healing from the pulpit on a regular basis, hosting conferences on healing, bringing in special speakers, etc. In every way, show people what a lifestyle of healing could look like.

How to Build Healing Ministry Structure

We provide or recommend trusted professional counselors to our people.

> *"I have seen his ways, and will heal him;*
> *I will also lead him,*
> *And restore comforts to him*
> *And to his mourners."*
> *— Isaiah 57:18*

One of the key roles of every church is to provide different kinds of healing opportunities for its members. Some churches create counseling centers; some have specialty small groups that deal with certain kinds of past hurts or addictive behaviors. Some have large group healing rooms or ministries dedicated to inner healing. We encourage you to build ministries to meet the healing needs in your church.

1. Train your leaders in healing.
Who in your church is gifted in this area of healing and mercy?
Equip them in a way that will benefit the people in their spheres
of influence.

2. Maintain a victorious perspective.
Take steps to recognize and learn the authority you have, so you
can do what Jesus did on the earth (see Acts 10:38).

3. Keep your vision for healing before the people.
Flood your church with testimonies of healing. In everything you
do, present truth in such a way that those who are hurting can
see Jesus and move toward purity and wholeness.

How to Build Healing Ministry Leadership

We provide specialized ministry to free people from spiritual
bondage.

> *"For I am the Lord who heals you."*
> — *Exodus 15:26*

Every church should have in its arsenal a place of healing and
restoration for its members. Fill your church with teachings and
resources on how to pray for healing, deliverance and comfort,
and find people who are actively walking in these things. If
possible, try to create income streams for them so they are able
to support themselves in this ministry—that is how important it is
to have healers readily available to your church body

As a leader, look at your congregation and see which individuals
have a calling for healing. As you preach on the topic, put out the
call and see who responds. Who loves well? Who wants to
comfort others? Who is known in your church as someone who
cares and nurtures and brings healing?

HEALING MINISTRY

The more you can identify these people and begin to pour into them, the more fruitful your ministry will be as a church and the healthier the body will be in general.

INTERGENERATIONAL MINISTRY

We value the partnership of generations for maximum impact.

You know how we exhorted, and comforted, and charged every one of you, as a father does his own children, that you would walk worthy of God who calls you into His own kingdom and glory.
— *1 Thessalonians 2:11–12*

We live in an individualized society that fully believes the motto, "I can do it by myself." We glorify the self-made man or woman; however, as we begin to examine history, we realize that our degree of individualization is on the extreme side of the pendulum. It is time to take a step back and experience biblical, integrous Christianity that sees the Church as God sees it: as a family.

At Pastor's Coach, we believe you cannot fully thrive as a church without intergenerational connection. As each age group in your church supports, honors, cares for one another and works together in harmony, your church will see Heaven come to earth in a major way. The three age groups in any church are your emerging (young) leaders, midlevel leaders (people in their 30s and 40s) and older leaders.

Intergenerational Ministry and the Culture of Honor

In his first epistle, the apostle John addresses different levels of maturity. He writes to the "children," whose sins are forgiven; to the "young men," who know God's Word and have overcome the wicked one; and finally to the "fathers," who know Him who is from the beginning. Three generations are presented, and each has something incredible to offer the others.

The idea of spiritual generations dovetails with the reality of age. Every church has older and younger saints, spiritual parents and spiritual children. You will have older believers in your church, as well as believers in their teens, 20s, 30s and so forth. How do you work with all of them? How do you create a sense of synergy between the generations so you can maximize God's purpose?

The main step is to emphasize a culture of honor. Sometimes it is unfortunately easy to dishonor those who are older or younger. This almost automatic response can be traced back to the cultural changes of the 1960s when "generation gap" terminology began to be used. Dishonoring other generations came to be embedded in our society. Many of us have unknowingly perpetuated a legacy of generational brokenness, instead of genuinely appreciating those who belong to a different age group.

How do we build churches that foster true honor for each generation? First, we need to remember that every age has something to offer. The older generation gives us strength and wisdom. The middle generation's power and passion drive us forward, and the emerging generation offers innovation and a vital sense of newness. As we build opportunities for intergenerational partnership, we synthesize wisdom, perseverance and innovation. All of this comes together in new expressions of Kingdom reality that revolutionize the Body of Christ and help us become the Church Jesus wants us to be.

Second, communicate to your older believers that they aren't done yet. They can make a huge difference in your congregation as spiritual grandparents. As a pastor, you have a responsibility to honor the older people in your midst and give them positions of visibility and influence. Speak with your midlevel and emerging leaders, and establish a mentoring process where there is mutual respect for the generations and appreciation for one another. This allows your church to become a full, thriving expression of Jesus Christ that brings transformation to your region. God calls Himself the God of Abraham, Isaac and Jacob—He is the God of generations.

The Ship Analogy

Intergenerational partnership is similar to a large sailing vessel that has multiple large sails and a deep keel. You have a tremendous amount of power to harness the wind—but if you don't have a deep keel, the wind will cause the ship to topple.

Unfortunately, a lack of "depth" is why many ministries fail. They have a significant potential for velocity...but not much depth. Your older leaders can act like the keel of a boat and establish a vertical sense of torque. They offer leverage that allows the wind to push hard into the sails without causing the boat to capsize. They have depth, experience and a sense of ballast that goes down into the depths of the water. Only in intergenerational partnership can maximum velocity be realized.

How to Build Intergenerational Vision

We help every generation to grow, serve and be served.

> *"And he will turn*
> *The hearts of the fathers to the children,*
> *And the hearts of the children to their fathers."*
> — *Malachi 4:6*

In 1 Kings 19, Elijah was emotionally broken. He had just experienced an incredible victory over the prophets of Baal, but then Jezebel threatened his life and he dropped into a depression. The Lord spoke to him in a still, small voice: "What are you doing here, Elijah?" Essentially, He was asking, "Why are you depressed?" The solution God gave Elijah was to mentor the next generation. He told him (this is a paraphrase), "Go and find Elisha, put your cloak upon him and raise him up as a prophet in your place." As a pastor, you have the power to communicate stories and ideas like this one to your people and promote a vision of unity in the generations.

How to Spread Intergenerational Vision in Your Church:
1. Speak about it from the pulpit.
2. Model it in the ways you set up your leadership team.
3. Create opportunities for younger leaders to be mentored by older leaders in your church.

As you do these things, the DNA of the Kingdom is passed from generation to generation, and the glory and beauty of Heaven are manifested on earth.

How to Build Intergenerational Culture

We value all ages for the unique contribution they make.

> *"But when he was still a great way off, his father saw him and had compassion, and ran and fell on his neck and kissed him."*
> — *Luke 15:20*

One of the keys to a thriving church is making sure members of all ages are valued and that their contribution is respected. As a pastor, you can build a culture that will propel your movement into powerful, amazing synergy.

As you seek to generate a culture of intergenerational partnership, you need three components: healthy values, priorities and practices.

1. Values that support intergenerational partnership
Integrity allows a church to honor God's purpose for every age level. Also, a church should value the strength gained through the wisdom of age, in addition to the innovation and sense of vitality found in the emerging age group.

2. Priorities of intergenerational partnership
Talk about intergenerational partnership and celebrate it from the pulpit on a regular basis. Keep it at the forefront of people's minds and show them what it can look like.

3. Make intergenerational partnership a daily practice in your church.
Make your home and ministry groups inclusive, so they involve different generational levels.

How to Build Intergenerational Lifestyle

We encourage everyone to mentor others and be mentored. And behold, the Lord stood above it and said: "I am the Lord God of Abraham your father and the God of Isaac; the land on which you lie I will give to you and your descendants."
— Genesis 28:13

Our society communicates, "The older you get, the less relevant you become." It is common for older people to feel more and more marginalized over time, and we can't have that mindset in the church. Some of the best ministry can be done by the elder community. People over 60 have a *huge* impact on the Body of Christ and the purposes of God for a region. We want to make sure our older members do not feel marginalized or irrelevant.

Let's look at three steps that will help us build a lifestyle of intergenerational partnership in our churches.

1. Give your elder leaders examples of intergenerational partnership.
Make certain the elder members of your congregation know the biblical stories that display intergenerational partnership, and show them how you, personally, have benefited from mentors.

2. Teach your elder leaders how to communicate.
Teach your elder leaders how to communicate with the younger generation.

3. Practice intergenerational partnership.
It may be necessary to bring the different generations together and let them practice interacting in partnership.

How to Build Intergenerational Structure

We connect older and younger leaders to pioneer new ministries together.

> *And the Lord appeared to him the same night and said, "I am the God of your father Abraham; do not fear, for I am with you. I will bless you and multiply your descendants for My servant Abraham's sake."*
> — *Genesis 26:24*

God is the God of Abraham, Isaac and Jacob—He is the God of generations, and every church needs a plan for helping the generations partner together.

1. Create hybrid teams.
Make intergenerational partnership part of the standard pioneering process in your church. Older leaders will help provide the strength, depth of wisdom and maturity needed for a new ministry.

2. Have leaders train up leaders.
In every ministry or group offered by your church, the leader should be training up her replacement to honor, respect and learn wisdom from older leaders.

3. Encourage small groups.
Don't neglect the power of small groups as a primary delivery system for every aspect of Christ. Make sure your people are invested in small groups, communicating with each other and processing intergenerational partnership together as a normal part of their Christian life/community experience. Make intergenerational partnership a priority in your own life.

How to Build Intergenerational Leadership

We connect older and younger leaders to minister together.

*And the things that you have heard from me among
many witnesses, commit these to faithful men who will
be able to teach others also.*
— 2 Timothy 2:2

How many generations are described in 2 Timothy 2:2? Four, if you count Paul. Paul was speaking to his son, who would speak to faithful men, who would teach others also. Paul was saying, "You've got to guard these things you've seen me do and learned from me. Pass them on to the next generation—multiply yourself into faithful men, who will multiply themselves into other people."

Multiplication is how the Body of Christ grows. It is the spiritual version of the original commandment given in Genesis, those four amazing statements: Be fruitful, multiply, fill the earth, subdue it. Intergenerational multiplication is the way God intends to change the world, and it begins as the different generations choose to partner together.

Make intergenerational partnership a foundation point in every team and ministry you build. Let people see how much this type of partnership matters to you, and remember that no matter how much you teach on this topic, nothing can replace your personal coaching as combined teams of older and younger leaders pioneer a new relationship and blend two age groups in wisdom and harmony.

The first function of every job description in a church should be to recruit and raise up its replacement. Your first job as a leader is to raise up the next leader. In this way the church grows, and you grow, and the life of God fills your city and region. As much as possible, build leadership development into every branch of your church. As John Wimber, founder of the Vineyard

Movement, said, "I never pay someone to do a job. I only pay those who can get others to do a job." Help your leaders learn to *identify, recruit, train, deploy, monitor* and *nurture* new leaders as their first priority. In the process, your whole church becomes an incubator for leadership.

Conclusion

Let's do the best we can to fulfill the great commission – by using ALL the gifts, equipping and mobilizing ALL the saints, using ALL legitimate means at our disposal, being totally flexible and willing to change ALL of our what we do as directed by the Lord, reaching out to ALL segments of society... beginning with ALL of our leaders – helping them fulfill their calling, empowered by the Spirit so we can truly be the New Testament Church expressed in New Reformation churches.